ANIMAL
Spider
DIARIES

STEVE PARKER

QEB

Copyright © QEB Publishing 2014

First published in the United States in 2014 by
QEB Publishing, Inc.
3 Wrigley, Suite A
Irvine, CA 92618
www.qed-publishing.co.uk

A CIP record for this book is available from the Library of Congress.

ISBN 978 1 60992 252 8

Editor Carey Scott
Illustrator Peter David Scott
Designer Dave Ball
Editorial Assistant Tasha Percy
Managing Editor Victoria Garrard

Printed and bound in China

Photo Credits
Key: t = top, b = bottom, l = left, r = right, c = center,
FC = front cover, BC = back cover.
Alamy images Nurlan Kalchinov 15t; **Corbis** Adam Jones 7t, Wim Klomp/Foto
Natura/Minden Pictures 29t; **Getty Images** Oxford Scientific 7b; **Shutterstock**
Cathy Keifer 28b, Vaclav Volrab 27b, Ana de Sousa, Luminis, Peter Jochems,
Peter Jilek & Marina & Natasha Dementeva, all background images

Contents

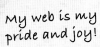

My web is my pride and joy!

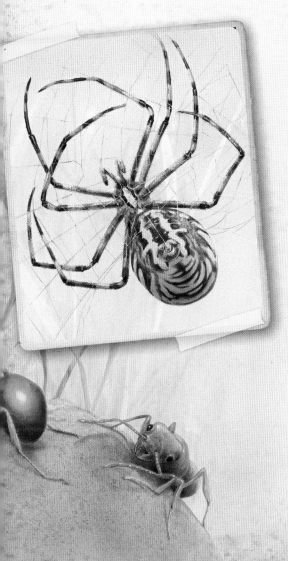

Web Sites

Heavy rain wrecked my last web, so I need a new one. Great, I love weaving! However, the last three of my brilliantly made silken nets caught nothing. So I'm on the lookout for a new place to spin my sticky trap. I need a new web site!

I'll climb higher for a better view.

Between upright stems of tall grasses might be a good spot for my new web.

Garden Orb-Web Spider

Group Arachnids—spiders, scorpions, mites, ticks

Adult body length
   Male 0.2-0.4 inches
   Female 0.5-1.2 inches

Habitat Gardens, parks, woods, grass

Food Flies, gnats, moths, beetles, similar small creatures

Features Female has a bright-striped body, perhaps also stripy legs. Male has a plainer body with fewer markings.

Before the rainstorm yesterday, my web had lasted three days—almost a record for me. Since then I've been looking around The Garden with my eight beady eyes for suitable places. The Giants of The Garden have even made some possible web sites for me. How thoughtful of them.

I like to spend time selecting the best position for my circular or orb-shaped web. Not too high, yet not too low. A gap between branches or bushes, where victims fly through, is usually successful. They hardly notice my super-fine silk strands and they soon become another delicious meal!

I could make my web across this hole in the Giant's wooden box.

Or perhaps here among leaves in a garden bush. . .

. . . or between these hard, cold branches.

My New Web

This site between two sets of grass stems looks just right. Time to get weaving! When I was tiny, my webs were so untidy. But I learned from the Ultimate Spider WIY (Weave-It-Yourself) instruction book.

The sticky spirals will trap tiny insects.

Radials are the base of my web.

That book was useful when I was a beginner. Now I'm growing up, I've progressed to expert level. I'm not boasting, but I really do make the biggest, tidiest, neatest webs in all of The Garden. In fact, I may write an advanced WIY book, to help those who are less skilled than me.

WEB MAKING: STEP-BY-STEP

Remember that web-weaving depends not only on physical skills. You will have setbacks so you need a positive approach and good mental attitude. One of the most famous spider sayings is: "If at first you don't succeed, spin, spin again."

1 Upwind of your web site, let the breeze drift a sticky strand so it catches the other side. Pull it tight.

The first strand

2 From each anchor point, make spoke-like strands, called radials, to run into the web's center, or hub.

Three radials

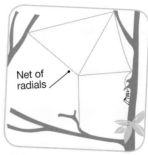

3 Position radials in different directions between the main frame and the hub. Make sure you pull them tight.

Net of radials

4 The first spiral goes around at an ever-increasing distance from the hub. Then lay the second sticky spiral.

First spiral in place

Not all spiders make wheel-shaped webs. Fang produces a funnel-shaped web. Stupid bugs walk into the wide end and keep going, right into Fang's . . . fangs. How dumb are they!

Snap the trapdoor spider makes a hinged door from silk, lays tripline strands around it, and waits in her nest burrow below. When a small creature touches a line, out she comes!

7

Watch 'n' Wait

*B*eing an orb-weaver has its ups and downs. One moment I'm busy web-weaving, then I wait for ages to catch something. Still, it gives me time to chat to other creatures and to learn more about myself.

My best friend Clever "H" the harvestman says all spiders have eight legs. She knows other eight-legged creatures too, like mites and ticks. We are all called ~~araknits~~ arachnids. A mite once lived on me and bit me. Horrible!

My abdomen contains my silk-making parts, called spinnerets.

My front end or head-thorax.

Tiny, sticky hairs on my legs help me walk up surfaces. No wonder they are called smart hairs!

My eight-legged family

SCORPIONS
Front and rear are dangerous! The large pincers grab prey or nip enemies. The curled tail has a sharp stinger at the end to jab deadly venom into victims.

Stinging tail

Large pincers

SUN SPIDERS
Also called camel spiders or solifuges, these have long "feelers" and powerful fangs. They live in hot places, especially deserts, lack venom or silk, but run super-fast.

Long body

Fierce fangs

Long feeler-like palps

While waiting, I chatted to Ant. I noticed I have two body parts—one with my head and eight legs, the other with my inner bits. Ant has three body parts, but only six legs! So she's not an arachnid like me, she's an insect.

Ant has antennae.

Ant's middle part is called her thorax.

Ant's abdomen.

MITES

Some mites are parasites, sucking blood from larger animals. Others roam around looking for any tiny scraps of food. Mites live everywhere except in the sea and Antarctica.

Feeler or palp

Needle-like mouthparts

Jointed legs, like all arachnids

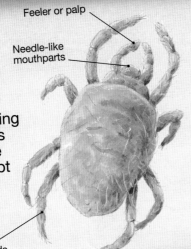

TICKS

These blood-sucking parasites live on all kinds of host animals, from furry mammals to feathery birds and even scaly reptiles. Like mites, most are even tinier than this "o."

Fat body full of blood

Front leg can detect nearby host

Claws cling to host

Making Repairs

My web yesterday was superb. But it caught nothing. It was too cold for most flying bugs. So I ate the web, as usual, to recycle its materials and build my next one.

Grass stem is a good support. →

Nooooo! Stag has walked straight through my new web. He looks fierce but his huge jaws are just for pushing around rival males and impressing females. They hardly bite at all.

Stag Beetle

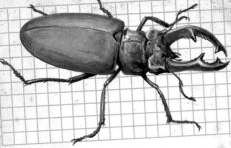

Group Insects—beetles

Adult length Male up to 3.9 inches including "antlers", female up to 2 inches

Habitat Woods, forests, parks, gardens

Food Larva (grub) eats rotting wood, adult sips juices from ripe fruits

Features Male has massive jaws shaped like antlers of a stag, or male deer, female's are much smaller but bite harder

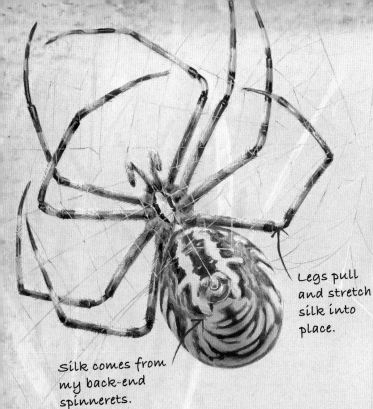

Legs pull and stretch silk into place.

Silk comes from my back-end spinnerets.

Look at the tears Stag left!

Stag was too big for me to attack, and easily escaped my sticky trap. He's done a lot of damage to my web. I'd better hurry up with some repairs. I hope I catch something soon, because I'm getting hungry.

SILK STRENGTH
How Does Spider Silk Compare?

As we all know, spiders make different kinds of silk for different jobs. See how the silk used for making the web's main frame compares with the strongest human-made materials:

	WEIGHT	STRENGTH	STRETCH
SPIDER SILK	Low	High	High
NYLON THREAD	Medium	Medium	Medium
STEEL WIRE	High	Medium	Low

SELECT-A-SILK

I use different silks for all these things:

1. Orb-web frame.

2. Web radials (spokes).

3. Non-sticky web spiral.

4. Sticky spiral for web.

5. Wrapping up victims.

6. Safety lines on the move.

7. Cocoon to wrap up eggs.

Spidery Friends

After waiting for hours in my web and catching nothing, I decided to go for a walk. It helps to stretch my eight legs. Also I can catch up on The Garden gossip.

Wolf has two big eyes and six small ones.

First I met my best friend, Clever "H." A harvestman is not exactly a true spider, but a very close cousin. She has a tiny body and eight mega-thin legs, but no silk or venom.

Next up was Wolf. He does not spin a web, but catches prey by running and leaping onto it. Wolf has fantastic eyesight— even better than mine.

Long, strong legs for fast chasing.

Air bubble between legs.

"H"'s body hangs down between her long legs.

Strolling past the pond, I chatted with Aqua the water spider. She comes to the surface to take air bubbles down to her underwater nest, where she lives and eats.

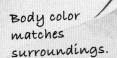

Body color matches surroundings.

Crab spider matches the color of the flower petals where she waits for prey. Clever "H" calls this ~~comerflarge~~ camouflage. Bugs like butterflies come to sip the flower's nectar, and Crab makes her move.

Red-Kneed Tarantula

Group Arachnids—spiders, scorpions, mites, ticks

Adult body length 4 inches

Leg span 6.7 inches

Habitat The House, or in tropical places and deserts

Food Any small animals, from little bugs to other spiders, frogs, lizards, and mice

Features Large size, hairy body and legs, multi-striped legs

Long hairs on body.

Red leg stripes.

My new friend Tara used to live in The House. She escaped but now she has regrets. She says The Garden is too cold and has none of her natural foods, like tropical insects.

Flying Feast

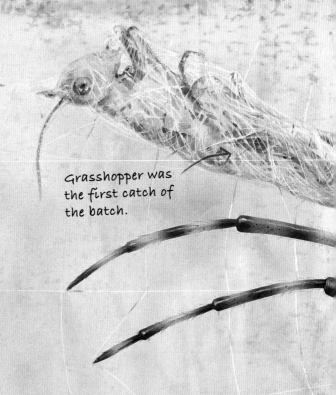

You wait and wait—then three come together! My latest, best-ever web has trapped a young grasshopper, a fly, and a ladybug. In a minute I'll race over and tackle the ladybug.

Grasshopper was the first catch of the batch.

WHAT I ATE LAST MONTH

1. A brown cricket.

2. A badly wounded bee that had stung another animal and so couldn't sting me.

3. A yellow butterfly.

4. Yet another brown moth from The Park.

I've already dealt with the fly and grasshopper. I squirted my venom into them with my fangs. This stopped them moving. Then I wrapped them up tightly in silk and left them to eat later. Yum!

I've never caught a ladybug before. I'm worried about its bright colors and patterns. Usually these warn of problems. Colorful creatures either sting or bite, or they taste horrible and make you sick.

Maybe that's why I have bright stripes, to let enemies know I can bite them. One of my nicknames is "wasp spider." Bees and wasps also have similar colors to warn about their sting.

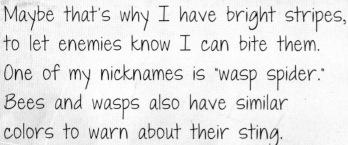

Spare prey packaged in strong silk.

Curved, sharp, fangs.

My venom is in the fang's bendy base.

I use my legs to wrap up prey.

I bit the grasshopper and fly with just enough venom so they cannot move but they are still alive. The creatures I eat are more delicious when not quite dead. But, er, I'm still worried about this colorful ladybug. Maybe I'll ask Clever "H" what to do...

Fly is trapped inside my silk wrapper.

Under Attack

Today was a total nightmare! On my new, improved web, I spied Liz the Lizard sneaking up on me between the leaves. That was the first of several attempts on my life. Luckily, using my great survival talents, I managed to avoid them all.

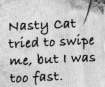

Nasty Cat tried to swipe me, but I was too fast.

web-shaking slowed Liz, but I had to make a break for it.

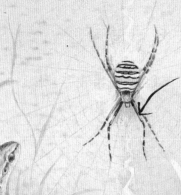

Thrush's peck only just missed me.

Liz flicked out her long tongue and looked hungry. I shook my web, like I usually do to warn off enemies. Liz stopped—then re-started.
I shook harder to gain time, leaped away and ran. Then Shrew, Thrush, and Nasty Cat almost caught me, too. Yikes!

I bared my fangs at Shrew.

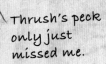

I headed to The Pond. There was Frog, watching with bulging eyes, long tongue ready to shoot out. I swerved amazingly away from Frog and ran expertly toward The Fence. Then a horrible wasp saw me! They kill spiders and lay eggs on us, so their babies can eat us!

Song Thrush

Group	Birds—thrushes and blackbirds
Adult length	8.7 inches
Wingspan	13 inches
Habitat	Woods, gardens, parks, scrub
Food	Any small animals such as worms, insects, and spiders, also fruits
Features	Spotty chest, sharp beak, loud musical songs

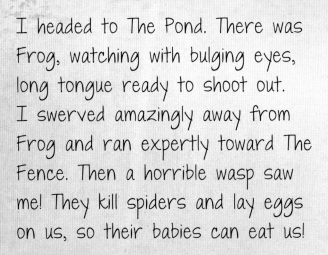

Frog would swallow me whole.

I headed for The Fence.

A spider-hunting wasp swooped, but I jumped away.

I climbed The Fence.

I'm safe! Dark and cool at long last.

On the move, I always make a silk strand for my safety line. To jump away from the wasp, I fixed my line to The Fence and swiftly lowered myself down it. Finally I was safe in a pile of short, lying-down trees. Phew!

A Strange Place

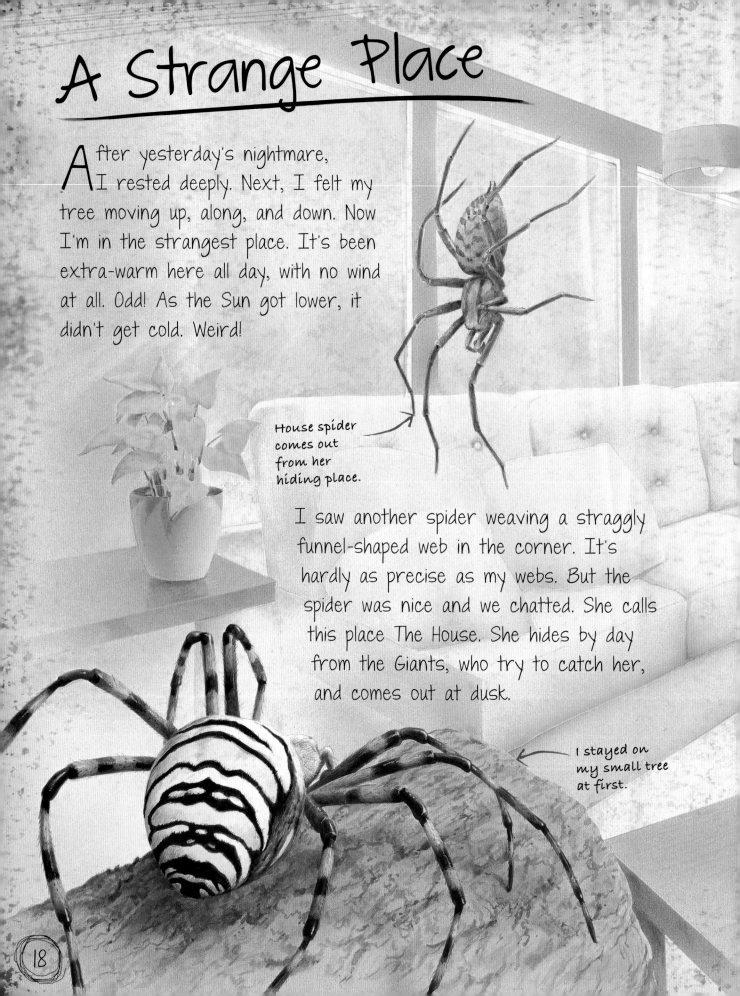

After yesterday's nightmare, I rested deeply. Next, I felt my tree moving up, along, and down. Now I'm in the strangest place. It's been extra-warm here all day, with no wind at all. Odd! As the Sun got lower, it didn't get cold. Weird!

House spider comes out from her hiding place.

I saw another spider weaving a straggly funnel-shaped web in the corner. It's hardly as precise as my webs. But the spider was nice and we chatted. She calls this place The House. She hides by day from the Giants, who try to catch her, and comes out at dusk.

I stayed on my small tree at first.

One of the Giants must have found Tara and brought her back to The House, because there she was! She looked much better in her tank—well-fed and hairs combed. Why do the Giants like Tara and dislike the House Spider?

House Spider

Group Arachnids—spiders, scorpions, mites, ticks

Adult body length 0.4–0.8 inches

Leg span 1.6–2.4 inches

Habitat Varied—from houses, cellars, garages, and sheds to gardens, parks, and woods

Food Flies and other insects, other spiders, mites, ticks

Features Funnel-shaped web. Male has smaller body and longer legs

---

84 *ULTIMATE SPIDER TIPS: Tarantulas*

RED-KNEED TARANTULA
Care instructions
Container: Glass or plastic tank.
Contents: Clean sandy soil, bark, stones, twigs, hiding and basking sites.
Temperature: 75–80 °F.
Humidity: Medium (use a water dish, clean and filled).
Food: Crickets, locusts, mealworms, cockroaches, about 4–6 per week.

Tara's happy to be back in her tank.

Trapped!

The House spider warned me about the slippery white pit. But did I listen? No, I thought I knew everything. So I went exploring for the best place to spin a new web. Then, suddenly... Whoooah!

Even my smart hairs can't get me out of this pit.

I slid so quickly, with hardly time to leave a safety line. I just managed to press one onto the pit's side, but it did not stick. What the heck are these smooth walls made of?

PEST CONTROL
Harmless spiders help in houses by eating. . .

1. Houseflies and blowflies

2. Gnats, midges, mosquitoes

3. Other biting, stinging, germ-spreading pests

I was trapped for hours. Even with all my eight legs, I couldn't climb out. I had some water, and I ate a small ant that also slid in. But I got so hungry!

I drank water drips from this hole.

20

Gradually, it got dark, as usual. Then, instantly the Sun came on and a loud screaming noise frightened me. Next thing, a big sheet like a square, white leaf pushed under my legs.

The small round tank was lifted away . . .

. . . by one of the Giants.

A small version of Tara's tank was on top of me. I tried to push out but it was too strong. I felt myself lifted and carried. Then I sensed fresh air and familiar noises. Freedom at last. Thank you, Giant!

With a few bounds, I was freeeee!

Home Again

I'm soooo pleased my great adventure is over. I learned a lot, like how to listen to others who know best. Today I met Clever "H" and a few of The Garden's creatures, and caught up with more gossip.

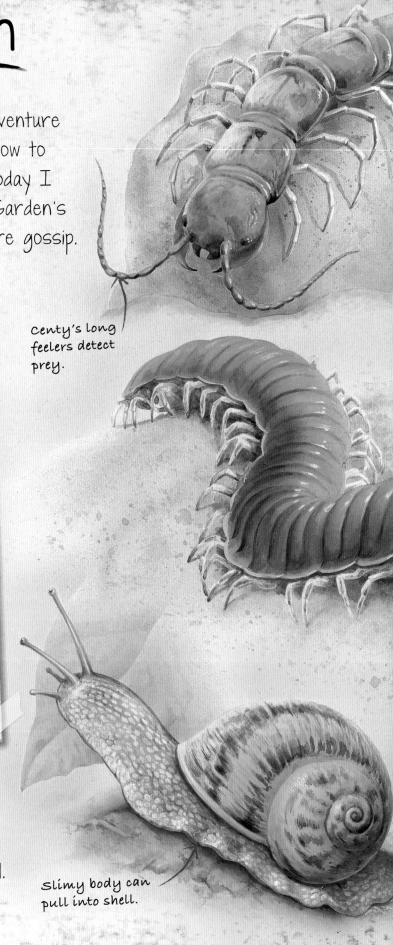

Centy's long feelers detect prey.

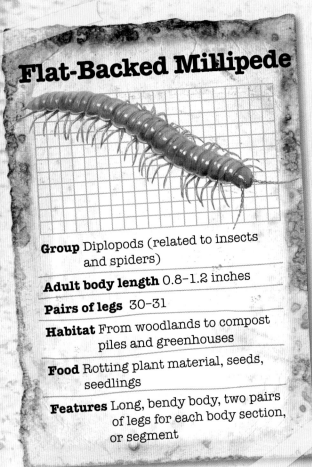

Flat-Backed Millipede

Group Diplopods (related to insects and spiders)

Adult body length 0.8–1.2 inches

Pairs of legs 30–31

Habitat From woodlands to compost piles and greenhouses

Food Rotting plant material, seeds, seedlings

Features Long, bendy body, two pairs of legs for each body section, or segment

Snail doesn't say much, or do much, or go far, or go fast. But ~~he~~ ~~she~~ it is very snug and protected in that hard ~~shall~~ shell. I wish I had a shell.

Slimy body can pull into shell.

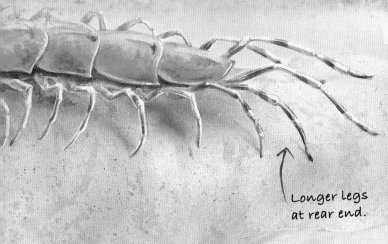

Longer legs at rear end.

Centy is a fast hunter, even quicker than me. However he has more legs—15 pairs. I wish I had as many.

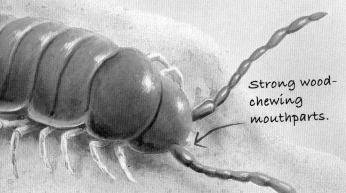

Strong wood-chewing mouthparts.

Woody the woodlouse hates the Sun, he likes dark dampness. All he eats is rotting bits and pieces. Boring! I'm glad I'm not Woody.

Milly has even more legs than Centy. But for some reason she's slower. To keep enemies away, she makes a horrible-smelling and foul-tasting fluid. Gross!

Woody has seven pairs of legs.

23

My Mate

Mating time is here again. That's a shame, because I much prefer weaving webs. But it's something all creatures do. So I started eight-eyeing a male who was hanging around.

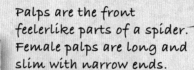

Palps are the front feelerlike parts of a spider. Female palps are long and slim with narrow ends.

Male spiders are usually smaller and duller than females. They are nervous and worried too, because if we females are hungry after mating we might eat them!

The male's palps are short with wide, clublike ends.

Male is much less colorful than me.

This is where I bit off his leg.

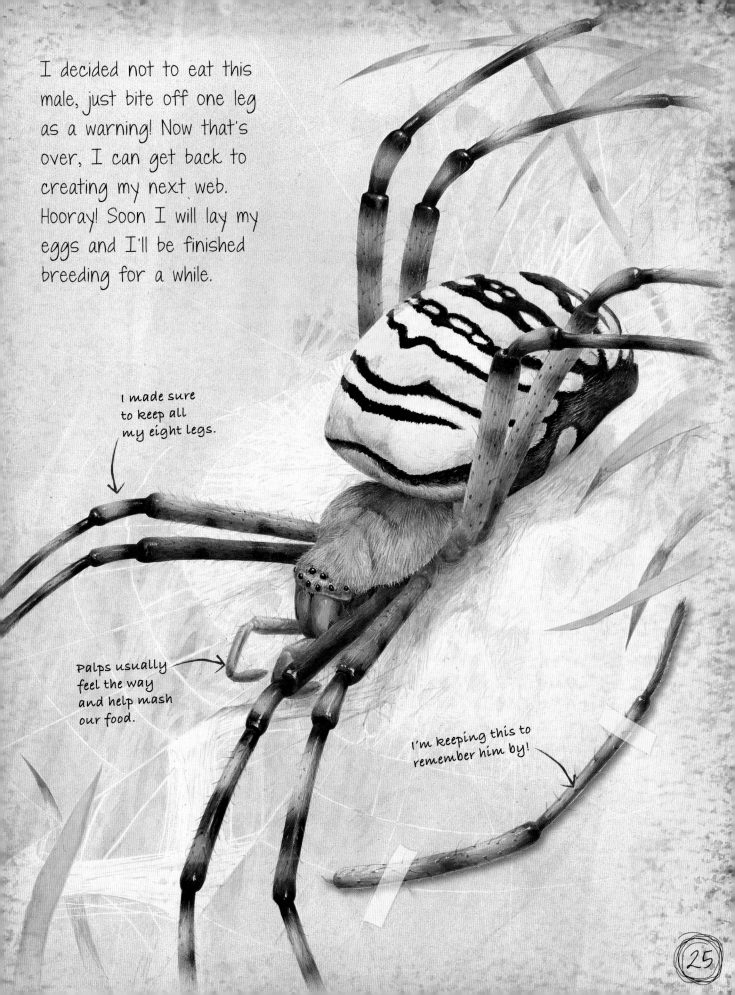

I decided not to eat this male, just bite off one leg as a warning! Now that's over, I can get back to creating my next web. Hooray! Soon I will lay my eggs and I'll be finished breeding for a while.

I made sure to keep all my eight legs.

Palps usually feel the way and help mash our food.

I'm keeping this to remember him by!

Spiderlings Go!

A month after mating, it's time to lay my eggs. I have felt so big and bloated, I will be pleased to get rid of them. It feels like there are hundreds of eggs—and there are!

I hang the cocoon from a strong twig or leaf.

Cocoon silk is extra-thick and long-lasting.

I guard the cocoon for as long as I can.

Animal parents try to give their offspring the best start. So I make sure the eggs are in a safe place, like under a leaf or in a quiet corner. Then I spin a special kind of silk into a casing around them, called a ~~cuckoon~~ cocoon.

Off they go to spin their first webs.

The spiderlings bite their way out of the cocoon.

I stay near the cocoon and protect it. But as my ~~mussels~~ muscles get colder, I can hardly move. Like most spiders in winter, I'll find a little hideaway for my Long Sleep.

Next spring, the babies will be on their own. When I was a spiderling, the world seemed so huge and dangerous. I can't look after them all. I may not even be here! But my diary will be, so reading it will help them.

Happy Family Photo (taken on my 8-eye-phone).

A New Me!

It's been a good year. I've had excellent adventures, caught hundreds of insects, and most of all taken web-making to a new level. Now that I've laid my eggs, I've just a few more jobs to do before a very Long Sleep.

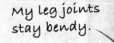
My leg joints stay bendy.

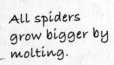
All spiders grow bigger by molting.

First, I will find somewhere quiet and safe, because it's time for me to shed or molt my old skin. It has become too small so I will wriggle out of it. My whole outer layer will come off—even the hard covers of my fangs. I will be spongy and soft-fanged for a while and unable to feed so will have to hide.

Bye-bye skin, you were a good one.

I will then grow larger and stronger before my new skin hardens. Then I'll weave a truly tremendous web and catch and eat lots, before I settle down for my Long Sleep in the cold winter.

Autumn dewdrops make my web even more beautiful.

What They Say About Me

My diary describes what I think of all the creatures I meet. But what do they think about me? Let's find out . . .

Stag Beetle

> " I'm too big, strong and hard to be worried by Spider's fangs. But I do admire the webs. They look so great. As Spider keeps telling us . . . "

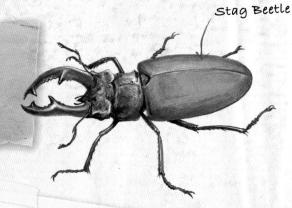

Millipede

> " Spider is always boasting about her wonderful webs. That really annoys me. Anyway, more legs means more intelligence, so I'm smartest. "

> " After being so helpful when I got lost in The Garden, it was awful to see Spider trapped in The House. But the kind Giants who look after me rescued her. "

Tarantula

House Spider

> " Spider and I both have venomous fangs. We have the same tastes too—any small insects we can catch. So usually we avoid each other. "

> " I tried to warn Spider about the slippery pit, but she wouldn't listen. Also, why do Giants care for Tara and rescue Spider—but try to squish me? So unfair! "

Centipede

Tricky Terms

Abdomen The rearmost body part containing most of the guts. A spider's abdomen is the second part of its body.

Antennae Feelers that detect touch, movement, smells, and tastes. Spiders lack antennae.

Arachnid An animal that has eight legs. There are around 80,000 different types of arachnids, including spiders.

Camouflage Merging with the shapes, colors, and patterns of the surroundings, to be less noticed.

Cocoon A case or container of threads made by a spider, insect, millipede, or similar creature.

Fang A long, sharp tooth. Spiders use their fangs to inject venom into their prey.

Hub In a spider's web, the center area where the radials join and the spirals start or finish.

Insect An animal with a head, thorax, abdomen, and six legs. There could be as many as 10 million types of insects.

Larva The wormlike young of insects and some other animals. Also called a grub.

Molt Shed or cast off a spider's old body covering or skin, usually to grow bigger before the new one hardens.

Palps Also called pedipalps, these are a spider's arms, used to feel the way and to mash up food.

Parasite An animal that lives on another animal, the host, causing it harm.

Smart hairs Tiny, sticky hairs on a spider's feet that enable it to walk on walls and ceilings.

Radials In a spider's web, the spokelike silk strands that run from anchor points into the center, or hub.

Spiderlings Baby spiders.

Spinnerets Bendy, fingerlike parts at the rear end of a spider's body, where liquid silk comes out before it hardens. Most spiders have six spinnerets.

Spirals In a spider's web, the silk strands that connect the radials, going around and around inward or outward to make a spiral shape.

Thorax A body part with the heart and, in spiders and insects, legs too. In spiders, the head is also part of the thorax.

Venom A harmful substance jabbed into a victim with sharp body parts such as fangs. Venom causes pain, inability to move, or even death.

> I've tried to catch Spider many times, but no luck yet. Although if I did succeed, The Garden would lack the touch of glamour that Spider's wonderful webs bring.

Song Thrush

Index